AF416562

Playground Grass

:::::::::::::::::::::::::::::::::

Haiku Options

~~~

Gary Hotham

Yiqralo Press

2022
~~~

Playground Grass: Haiku Options

Copyright ©2022 Gary Hotham

Revised

Yiqralo Press
Scaggsville
Maryland USA

IN OUR STATE NO ONE EVER

No one ever cared
how the rain looked. It wore
capers and long hair mostly and
sandals or gym shoes. It would
lounge along, testing puddles and dead
leaves and anything else it found friendly.

No one ever found
where the rain lived. It would
come on dark days, broad shouldered
over the Coast Range, and stay
casually chattering at intervals, often
through dinner and even late at night.

I followed it once,
east into the mountains. It leaned
and with a last pat it turned away
into one of those canyons no road
has found. It likes the dark, I thought,
and has a steady friend in the west wind.

No one ever helped
the rain, though, enough—oh,
travelers and children maybe, a little.
And some of us who held Scripture in mind,
or had old things to touch,
we held out a hand.

William Stafford

passing thru
the cracks in life
sunrise

leaving the ICU
everyone's breath
on their own

AIR

later in the meeting
rain stronger than
the agenda

the shadow
moving with all the others
a tree planted in her memory

night cools down the message
watching stars find
their places

moving thru space
the pole bean within
the grandson's reach

pushing dirt over seeds
flowers in the photo
on the package

dumped in a hole
water the grandson took
from the ocean

the wind's new strength
playground grass growing
taller

lifting
the overcast
the crow's caw caw caw

outlasting
another generation
a mountain higher than the others

early morning clouds
filling the window
your dent in the pillow

passing clouds
the bruise peeled off
the apple

low tide
the ocean drying out of
the driftwood

rain clearing away the tourists
stones older than
the ruins

more snow in the forecast
what the mirror had
leaves the room

losing interest
in the day's events
ripe tomatoes spoiling on the vine

hiking
shade the sun hasn't
found

day fades
water keeping water
on top

our last visit
the plane de-iced twice
before take off

soaking in the rain
stones picked out of
her garden

windows facing the street
rain making its way
thru the traffic

with the grandson
bird calls to
unseen birds

Sing to the Lord with thanksgiving;
    make melody to our God on the lyre!

He covers the heavens with clouds;
    he prepares rain for the earth;
    he makes grass grow on the hills.

He gives to the beasts their food,
    and to the young ravens that cry.

His delight is not in the strength of the horse,
    nor his pleasure in the legs of a man,

but the Lord takes pleasure in those who fear him,
    in those who hope in his steadfast love.

Psalm 147:7-11

The haiku were first published in the following:

Acorn
Akitsu Quarterly
Blithe Spirit (UK)
Hedgerow (UK)
Modern Haiku
Pinyon Review
Presence (UK)
Seashores (Ireland)
Solitary Plover
Tsuri-Doro

Author's Shadow Update

Photos

Front: Snowed-on-Reader, Scaggsville, Maryland, Jan 2022

Inside
1st: Tree Crawl, Scaggsville, Maryland, Nov 2022
2nd: Sign for Air, Longwood Gardens, Pennsylvania, Mar 2021
3rd: Pigeons on the Wires, Beverly, Massachusetts, Sep 2021
4th: 17 Year Cicada Shells, Scaggsville, Maryland, May 2021
5th: Honeybee on a Daisy, Scaggsville, Maryland, July 2021
6th: Tree and Lamp, Longwood Gardens, Pennsylvania, Mar 2021
7th: Icy Mailbox, Scaggsville, Maryland, Feb 2021
8th: Poet's Shadow Update, West Chester, Pennsylvania, Dec 2021

Back: Haiku Bear Critic in the Man Cave, Jan 2022

Quotes on back cover:

Herbert Butterfield, The Whig Interpretation of History, London:
G. Bell and Sons, Ltd, 1950, pages 65-66.

Malcolm Guite, The Word within the Words, Minneapolis:
Fortress Press, 2022, p. 14

Chapbooks in the 21st Century

Mannequins Dress for the Window: Haiku Secrets
Yiqralo Press 2021

Park Bench Memories: Haiku Tailwinds
Yiqralo Press 2020

Rightsizing the Universe: Haiku Theory
Yiqralo Press 2019

23
Longhouse 2019

Nothing More Happens in the 20th Century: Haiku Dangers
Pecan Grove Press 2011

Sand Over Sand
Longhouse 2009

Missed Appointment: The Haiku Art
Modest Proposal Chapbooks 2007

Haikus are easy
But sometimes they don't make sense
Refrigerator

www.ingramcontent.com/pod-product-compliance
Lightning Source LLC
Chambersburg PA
CBHW070326160726
47999CB00003B/1171